Anorexia Nervosa: Patient's Log Book

ANOREXIA NERVOSA:

PATIENT'S LOG BOOK

Based on the "St George's" approach to treatment

by

A H Crisp

Your name:

Copyright © 1995 by Psychology Press Ltd,
a member of the Taylor & Francis Group.

Reprinted 1997

Psychology Press Ltd, Publishers
27 Church Road
Hove, East Sussex
BN3 2FA
UK

British Library Cataloguing in Publication Data

A catalogue record for this book is available from the British Library

ISBN 0-86377-407-5

Cover by The Design Revolution
Typeset by HH Design
Printed and bound in the UK by BPC Wheatons Ltd, Exeter

THIS IS YOUR LOG BOOK

It is primarily designed to help you focus your feelings and thoughts and to record them and your experiences during treatment. Our aim, together with you and others such as your family, is to make them as constructive as possible. To escape from your anorexia, you and others close to you will need to develop new understandings and ways of relating and doing things.

The log book begins with a record of your initial visit to the clinic together with your parents and/or someone else close to you. There is a space for you to jot down your thoughts about that visit and to put in a copy of the letter you wrote indicating your wish to engage in treatment. This may help to remind you, from time to time, that there is part of you that does want to escape the grip of your illness. There is also a space for the name of the therapist and the dietician who will be involved with your treatment and, importantly, a place for you and your family to put your commitment to this treatment in writing by reading the brief introduction and then signing your log book. Next is the reading list of books which we think are relevant to your problem. After this comes a statement about your target weight, usually identified as being relevant to the age at which you developed your anorexia nervosa.

The log book is then divided into sections dealing with "Before Target Weight" and "After Target Weight". Firstly, there is an outline of the programme followed by pages which we hope will help you to look at yourself and others in a structured way. They cover many things but not, hopefully, everything, especially as you once again develop the individual side of your nature. At the end of each of these sections are pages on which it is intended that you can regularly review your progress both when you are by yourself and also when you are with those helping you.

At the end of the "book" there are personal diary pages.

Apart from the therapy and dietary advice sessions we will be asking you to do certain "homework". Your treatment is not just something done "to" you at intervals but is something you do, with periodic expert help. This homework will be explained to you at the outset and includes the use of this log book and a linked self-help book, and also some of the other books we have recommended.

2

Date of initial out-patient assessment: ....

Those who attended:　You　..

　　　　　　　　　　　Others　1. ....

(Put the names in here)　　2. ....

　　　　　　　　　　　　　　3. ....

　　　　　　　　　　　　　　4. ....

Name of the doctor/other person
who undertook the initial assessment
with you and your family　..

Why not jot down here some of your memories of your first assessment so
that you and your therapist can come back from time to time and reflect on
why you might have felt as you did

....

....

....

Name and signature of the therapist who ....
will facilitate your log book intervention

　　　　　　　　　　　　　　　　　..

Name of log book partner
(if different from above)　　　　..

Names of others involved　　　　..
(e.g. dietician, occupational
therapist)　　　　　　　　　　..

You and your family may all experience the psychotherapy that you become involved in as quite challenging and invasive. We believe you know this because we will have told you so but we would like you and any family members involved to commit yourselves here to this aspect of the treatment. You may all find that doing this now in this formal way will help you in the months to come when you are under strain and can look back to this point.

We all understand that we are engaging in psychotherapy and not only consent to this but agree to participate actively with the aim of solving the problems that are currently causing the anorexia nervosa.

Signed   ....
(person with anorexia nervosa)

Signed   ....

(   )

....

(   )

(family members)

READING LIST

We think and hope that the following books may be helpful to you and we would like you to try and read them whilst in treatment. Some have been selected because they are specifically about anorexia, others are about subjects that are related to anorexia nervosa in all or some people. One or two are now out of print but it should still be possible to obtain them through public libraries. The order in which you read them should be discussed with your therapist.

One book is rather different from the rest, and so we will mention it first :

Anorexia Nervosa and the Wish to Change

By   A H Crisp, N Joughin, C Halek, C Bowyer
                    Published by Lawrence Erlbaum Associates

This "self-help" book can be used by you during treatment. Whilst in treatment you are taking the same 30 steps in your attempt at full recovery, having undertaken to surrender to us your absolute control over your body weight. This, together with all the psychotherapy and your use of the log book, can allow you to concentrate on matters potentially having to do with freedom in other areas of your life and underlying your panic about weight gain and feelings of helplessness at normal weight, which are also covered in the "self-help" book.

We would like you to buy a copy, familiarise yourself with its contents, and keep it by you to refer to when you leave us, having perhaps by then highlighted parts of the text that seem important for you (there is also space for writing in the margins).

BOOKS ABOUT ANOREXIA NERVOSA

Anorexia Nervosa : Let Me Be

By   A H Crisp   Published by Lawrence Erlbaum Associates

Our general approach is reflected in detail in this book. It attempts to link the social, cultural, personal and physical aspects of the condition both in terms of its development and its treatment. Against this background, towards the end of the book, 10 patients, and sometimes their families, describe their own experiences of the condition. You may want to read these first. Then have a go at reading the book through. The author suggests that "Anorexia nervosa is a biological solution to an existential problem". What do you think?

The Golden Cage

By   Hilda Brüch   Published by Open Books

This book is a classic of its kind. We differ in our views only in degree from Dr. Brüch who presents anorexia nervosa as the "pursuit of thinness" as though this was a choice of identity rather than a flight to a refuge permitting no alternative. She also emphasises the primacy of food rather than body shape in her attempt to understand the factors that precede anorexia nervosa during childhood and to relate them to the illness. We suggest you read this alongside **Let Me Be**, searching out the differences and similarities of approach.

Anorexia Nervosa

By   R L Palmer   Published by Penguin Books

This is a very useful and comprehensive book which aims to help you make some sense of anorexia nervosa and hospital treatment. It is written by a doctor and concentrates largely on medical approaches to anorexia, but it doesn't do this in a narrow-minded way. It is easy to read and should help you and your family be better informed about anorexia.

6

The Anorexic Experience

By   Marilyn Lawrence   Published by The Women's Press

This book is written by a therapist at the Women's Therapy Centre in London. She has had a great deal of experience in working with women suffering from anorexia and her views are based on a feminist approach to the problems young women face in life. Her approach is in no way extreme and the book offers a useful, non-medical way of looking at anorexia. It is readable, informative and encouraging and includes plenty of examples of women's differing experiences of having anorexia. The book invites you to choose whether or not to tackle your difficulties and how to find a way of doing this that suits you, in a very supportive way.

The Art of Starvation

By   Sheila MacLeod   Published by Virago

This book should be seen as consisting of two parts. The first part involves Sheila MacLeod's very personal description of her childhood and the experiences she sees, with hindsight, as being important influences on her subsequent anorexia. Her account of family life and her school days is particularly evocative and well written. The second part of the book revolves around the author's own view of how and why people develop (choose) anorexia as a means of coping and self determination. In this she discusses theoretical issues, as well as her own attempts at recovery. This is quite technical at times, and generally harder going for the reader. Overall, it is a worthwhile book, which would probably benefit from being read around, and shortly after, the time of reaching target weight.

Eating Your Heart Out

By   Julia Buckroyd   Published by Optima Books

This book is about eating difficulties in general, not just anorexia, and it is aimed at helping you think about what underlies your eating disorder. It is easy to read and develops some of the ideas contained here. It should set you thinking!

BOOKS ABOUT FAMILIES AND RELATIONSHIPS

Families and How to Survive Them

By   Robin Skynner and John Cleese   Published by Methuen

This is a very popular and charming book which explains simply and clearly the process of development of the personality and how this is affected by the family's established patterns of communication.

It describes in an amusing and entertaining way basic psychological concepts. We highly recommend this book which has particular relevance to your attempts to understand your personality, your family relationships and the ways in which you relate to others.

Games People Play

By   E Berne   Published by Deutsch
            (Also available in paperback, published by Penguin Books)

This book is about the different ways in which people relate to each other. The author looks at them as "games" in which the participants "agree" to take on different roles according to what they hope to gain from their relationships. People tend to play similar roles even in different relationships. This book can help you look at the way you relate to others and how they in their turn relate, both to you and to other people. You may be able to find patterns of relating. The book is fairly scholarly, but is also intended for a wider audience.

BOOKS ABOUT SEXUALITY AND RELATIONSHIPS

First Love, First Sex: a Practical Guide to Relationships

By   Kaye Wellings   Published by Thorsons Publishing Group

This book is recommended by the Family Planning Association, and is a clear, comprehensive and readable guide to all aspects of intimate and sexual relationships. Although its title suggests it is a "beginners book", it nevertheless contains a lot of information of use to anyone who has anxieties about or difficulties with intimate relationships. It is full of illustrations and well worth buying for yourself.

Girls and Sex;
Boys and Sex

By   Wardell B Pomeroy   Published by Penguin

These books are written from years of experience of counselling young people on sexuality. They are direct and informative and aim to explore this area in an explicit and unembarrassed way. They are very readable and can help to allay a lot of anxieties about sexual feelings and behaviour.

Friday's Child

By   Carol Lee   Published by Thorsons Publishing Group

A personal account of sex education for teenagers in schools which is readable and particularly sensitive about the neglected male angle.

BOOKS ABOUT BECOMING AN ADULT

Everygirls' Lifeguide

By   Miriam Stoppard   Published by Dorling Kindersley

This book is informal and chatty and deals with many aspects of growing up, both physically and psychologically. It is well illustrated and easy to read. Its main fault is that it tries to cover too many areas at once, and we think that some of them are treated rather superficially, but it would do as an introduction.

A Woman in Your Own Right

By   Anne Dickson   Published by Quartet Books

This is a clearly written, informative book looking at ways in which one can become more assertive by developing clear and direct ways of communicating. Particular areas addressed are saying "no", handling criticism, managing the expression of anger, sexuality and assertiveness, and how body language conveys feelings.

If you are male, you can read this book with advantage. It will tell you how many women feel and it may also help you to define yourself better.

The Blind Side of Eden

By   Carol Lee   Published by Bloomsbury

This is a book about men and women written by a woman. It is perceptive, clear and uncompromising. It can help many of us get a firm, more accurate view of ourselves through such processes as telling us how others see us. Read the last page first and then be prepared to put your feet up.

BOOKS ON SEXUAL ABUSE

Sexual abuse has sometimes been experienced by people now suffering from anorexia. Because this is a subject which is especially difficult to approach, we are including some books which might help you in thinking about it, and eventually talking about it whether or not it has happened to you.

I KnowWwhy the Caged Bird Sings

By   Maya Angelou   Published by Virago

If I Should Die Before I Wake

By   Michelle Morris   Published by Black Swan

These two books are written by people who have personally experienced sexual abuse.

A Girl Like Abby

By   Hadley Irwin   Published by Plus Fiction

This book is a novel about sexual abuse and dealing with the experience.

10

Too Close Encounters and What to Do About Them

By   Rosemary Stones   Published by Piccadilly Press

This is a book about how to keep yourself safe and what to do if you find yourself in a dangerous or uncomfortable situation. It is easy to read and very practical in its approach.

BOOKS TO HELP WITH SOME OTHER PROBLEMS AND DIFFICULTIES ALSO ASSOCIATED WITH ANOREXIA NERVOSA

Frogs into Princes

By   R Bandler and J Grindler   Published by Real People Press

This book doesn't specifically address anorexia, but it is relevant to many issues arising later in your treatment. It presents a form of psychotherapy that emphasises how to change behaviour — as well as achieve understanding. Whilst intended for therapists, it's easy enough to read (after a difficult start) and chatty in style. Partly because of this it seems glib in making change sound *easy* — with which we don't agree — but there are plenty of ideas worth extracting.

Human Aggression

By   Anthony Storr   Published by Penguin

This book sets out to explain why anger and aggression evolved, and their value in many situations. It describes what happens to people when they are angry, and goes on to discuss how people are affected by anger when they can't express it.

It is a rather technical book, but we wanted to include something about this area of emotional experience because it's something anorectics usually have a lot of difficulty with. It is quite easy reading, and not long, so even if you find it hard to see yourself in the descriptions, give it a try.

Depression. The Way Out of Your Prison

By   Dorothy Rowe   Published by Routledge & Kegan Paul

At some weights you may be spared depression though anorexia nervosa itself can invoke depression because it is so handicapping and exhausting. However, as you gain weight or come out of anorexia nervosa you are certain to experience new feelings of hopelessness and helplessness. This can be frightening and it is likely that neither you nor your family have the skills to deal with such an episode. This book will help you recognise what is happening to you and what you can do about it. The book may also be useful to parents who are experiencing depression — as you begin to recover. If you feel that they are being helped then you can go on recovering.

USEFUL FICTION

There are very many novels written about relationships and feelings with which you might be able to identify and which you might find it helpful to read. We give just an introductory selection below.

The Secret Diary of Adrian Mole Aged 13 $^{3}/_{4}$

By   Sue Townsend   Published by Methuen

The Death of the Heart

By   Elizabeth Bowen   Published by Virago

The Summer After the Funeral

By   Jane Gardam   Published by Penguin

The Rainbow

By   D H Lawrence   Published by Penguin

The Catcher in the Rye

By   J D Salinger   Published by Penguin

OVERALL TREATMENT PROGRAMME

The treatment programme is going to involve you in engaging in dietary advice normally aimed at enabling you to gain weight in a predictable way. This is made possible by the accompanying psychological help which sets out to examine the basis of your panic about weight gain and its relationship to your sense of competence and self-esteem.

To this end you will be engaged in several phases of treatment, some of them preceding your achievement of target weight and some following on thereafter.

The number of specific sessions of treatment in which you will be involved will vary according to circumstances. These will include your own needs and also the resources of the unit caring for you. However many therapy sessions are involved, it will normally be the case that you remain in touch with the service and continue with a more diluted form of the treatment and your own "homework" for several years.

TARGET WEIGHT

If the goal of treatment is to try and liberate you from the grip of anorexia nervosa, then a target weight will have been identified which is the average weight of someone of your height and sex at the age at which your illness overwhelmed you. In other words, as you will learn from our self-help book and from **Let Me Be**, our aim is to slowly help you (and usually your family also) to begin to address once again the emotional issues and problems which were around at that time and which, since then, have been stifled. In one sense therefore the idea is that, in the first instance, you will be picking up the threads of life again as someone at that point of development.

Agreed age of onset ....

Height ....

On this basis your target weight is calculated
as being ....

BEFORE-TARGET WEIGHT PROGRAMME

The task for this initial stage of the programme is to gradually relinquish one's anorectic strategies and repertoire of control mechanisms in order to fulfill the aim of reaching the agreed target weight. The aim of the target weight is to try and foster development towards the age at which the problem started. This will mean preparing oneself to move through puberty again and the headings in the log book are in part intended to guide you in your experience and thinking about this very important developmental change. The log book headings also encompass the wider social and family environment and allow you to look at individual difficulties in each of these spheres. The psychotherapeutic process will endeavour in the out-patient sessions to facilitate this growth and development. The log book is your own personal record and a guide to help you in beginning to face these areas again. We suggest you date each entry.

Dietetic advice and support will buttress this log book work. You may have many questions about the frequency with which you weigh yourself, how you manage activity as well as diet. These questions can be tackled by using the information contained in the self-help book. Dietetic problems can be raised and discussed using the log book but it is important to be aware that the log book may then be taken over with dietetic issues. If this were the case, it should be recognised as an anorectic strategy to avoid dealing with the important conflicts that the other headings in the log book allude to.

To guide and support you in your endeavours of weight gain we recommend that you use the log book as prescribed in the following sections. On the following pages are titles of subjects which we believe to be particularly relevant to people with anorexia nervosa. We suggest that you briefly record each week your feelings and thoughts about each topic so that you can discuss them with your therapist and then take them into account with your reviews. We also encourage you to read extensively about anorexia nervosa. The self-help book and Let Me Be are two books that may help you to organise your thoughts and views.

At the end of this first section are pages which are used to structure reviews of your progress.

At the first review you need to agree a goal for each topic against which to rate any change in your recognition and understanding of yourself.

The final part of the pre-target weight section of the log book is the problems list. Some but not all of the problems listed may apply to you and it will be important for you with the therapist to change the list, if necessary, to best reflect your own individual difficulties. These problems may occur at different times and in different situations. This page can help you pinpoint these problems, consider the resources and strategies you can adopt to tackle these problems. These may change as you continue along the road to recovery.

14

THE MEANING OF MY SHAPE TO ME

THE MEANING OF MY SHAPE TO ME

THE TRIGGER(S) OF MY ILLNESS AND THEIR MEANING(S)

THE TRIGGER(S) OF MY ILLNESS AND THEIR MEANING(S)

MY FAMILY (OF ORIGIN) RELATIONSHIPS: BEFORE AND SINCE ANOREXIA NERVOSA

MY FAMILY (OF ORIGIN) RELATIONSHIPS: BEFORE AND SINCE ANOREXIA NERVOSA

MY SENSE OF SELF — SOCIAL

MY SENSE OF SELF — SOCIAL

MY SENSE OF SELF — SEXUAL

MY SENSE OF SELF — SEXUAL

24

RELATIONSHIP(S) WITH PARTNERS: BEFORE AND SINCE ANOREXIA NERVOSA

RELATIONSHIP(S) WITH PARTNERS: BEFORE AND SINCE ANOREXIA NERVOSA

THE ORIGINS OF MY ANXIETY

THE ORIGINS OF MY ANXIETY

MY USE OF AVOIDANCE TO DEAL WITH CONFLICT

MY USE OF AVOIDANCE TO DEAL WITH CONFLICT

MY FAMILY'S USE OF AVOIDANCE TO DEAL WITH CONFLICT

MY FAMILY'S USE OF AVOIDANCE TO DEAL WITH CONFLICT

32

MY OTHER MOODS

MY OTHER MOODS

WHY I APPROACH OTHERS IN THE WAY THAT I DO

WHY I APPROACH OTHERS IN THE WAY THAT I DO

MY PRESENT OR FUTURE CAREER; WHY I HAVE CHOSEN IT

MY PRESENT OR FUTURE CAREER; WHY I HAVE CHOSEN IT

MY RELATIONSHIPS WITH AUTHORITY

MY RELATIONSHIPS WITH AUTHORITY

MY IMPULSES AND THE WAY I MANAGE THEM

MY IMPULSES AND THE WAY I MANAGE THEM

DIFFICULTIES WITH MY CHOICE OF FOOD

DIFFICULTIES WITH MY CHOICE OF FOOD

NEW THINGS AND/OR SITUATIONS I WOULD LIKE TO TRY AND
EXPERIMENT WITH

NEW THINGS AND/OR SITUATIONS I WOULD LIKE TO TRY AND EXPERIMENT WITH

MY DIFFICULTY GAINING WEIGHT

MY DIFFICULTY GAINING WEIGHT

ANY OTHER PROBLEMS
Specify what the problem is:

....

ANY OTHER PROBLEMS
Specify what the problem is:

....

ANY OTHER PROBLEMS
Specify what the problem is:

....

ANY OTHER PROBLEMS
Specify what the problem is:

....

FIRST (BEFORE-TARGET WEIGHT) REVIEW (to be discussed with therapist)

DATE .... (insert the date for your next review now on the next review sheet)

MY RATING OF CHANGE IN ME:
1 = More of a problem than ever
2 = No real change
3 = Some improved recognition and understanding of this subject
4 = Much improved recognition and understanding of this subject

	RATING OF CHANGE				INDICATE IF DISCUSSED WITH LOG BOOK PARTNER
THE MEANING OF MY SHAPE TO ME	1	2	3	4	
THE TRIGGER(S) OF MY ILLNESS AND THEIR MEANING(S)	1	2	3	4	
MY FAMILY RELATIONSHIPS BEFORE AND SINCE ANOREXIA	1	2	3	4	
MY SENSE OF SELF: SOCIAL	1	2	3	4	
MY SENSE OF SELF: SEXUAL	1	2	3	4	
THE ORIGINS OF MY ANXIETY	1	2	3	4	
MY USE OF AVOIDANCE TO DEAL WITH CONFLICT	1	2	3	4	
MY FAMILY'S USE OF AVOIDANCE TO DEAL WITH CONFLICT	1	2	3	4	
MY OTHER MOODS	1	2	3	4	
WHY I APPROACH OTHERS IN THE WAY THAT I DO	1	2	3	4	
MY PRESENT OR FUTURE CAREER: WHY I HAVE CHOSEN IT	1	2	3	4	
MY RELATIONSHIPS WITH AUTHORITY	1	2	3	4	
MY IMPULSES AND THE WAY I MANAGE THEM	1	2	3	4	
DIFFICULTIES WITH MY CHOICE OF FOOD	1	2	3	4	
NEW THINGS/SITUATIONS I WOULD LIKE TO TRY	1	2	3	4	
MY DIFFICULTY GAINING/ MAINTAINING WEIGHT	1	2	3	4	
ANY OTHER PROBLEMS (PLEASE SPECIFY)	1	2	3	4	

....

WE SUGGEST YOU RAISE THESE THINGS IN ANY PART OF THE THERAPY

SECOND (BEFORE-TARGET WEIGHT) REVIEW (to be discussed with therapist)

DATE .... (insert the date for your next review now on the next review sheet)

MY RATING OF CHANGE IN ME:
1 = More of a problem than ever
2 = No real change
3 = Some improved recognition and understanding of this subject
4 = Much improved recognition and understanding of this subject

	RATING OF CHANGE	INDICATE IF DISCUSSED WITH LOG BOOK PARTNER
THE MEANING OF MY SHAPE TO ME	1 2 3 4	
THE TRIGGER(S) OF MY ILLNESS AND THEIR MEANING(S)	1 2 3 4	
MY FAMILY RELATIONSHIPS BEFORE AND SINCE ANOREXIA	1 2 3 4	
MY SENSE OF SELF: SOCIAL	1 2 3 4	
MY SENSE OF SELF: SEXUAL	1 2 3 4	
THE ORIGINS OF MY ANXIETY	1 2 3 4	
MY USE OF AVOIDANCE TO DEAL WITH CONFLICT	1 2 3 4	
MY FAMILY'S USE OF AVOIDANCE TO DEAL WITH CONFLICT	1 2 3 4	
MY OTHER MOODS	1 2 3 4	
WHY I APPROACH OTHERS IN THE WAY THAT I DO	1 2 3 4	
MY PRESENT OR FUTURE CAREER: WHY I HAVE CHOSEN IT	1 2 3 4	
MY RELATIONSHIPS WITH AUTHORITY	1 2 3 4	
MY IMPULSES AND THE WAY I MANAGE THEM	1 2 3 4	
DIFFICULTIES WITH MY CHOICE OF FOOD	1 2 3 4	
NEW THINGS/SITUATIONS I WOULD LIKE TO TRY	1 2 3 4	
MY DIFFICULTY GAINING/ MAINTAINING WEIGHT	1 2 3 4	
ANY OTHER PROBLEMS (PLEASE SPECIFY)	1 2 3 4	

....

WE SUGGEST YOU RAISE THESE THINGS IN ANY PART OF THE THERAPY

THIRD (BEFORE-TARGET WEIGHT) REVIEW (to be discussed with therapist)

DATE .... (insert the date for your next review now on the next review sheet)

MY RATING OF CHANGE IN ME:
    1 = More of a problem than ever
    2 = No real change
    3 = Some improved recognition and understanding of this subject
    4 = Much improved recognition and understanding of this subject

	RATING OF CHANGE				INDICATE IF DISCUSSED WITH LOG BOOK PARTNER
THE MEANING OF MY SHAPE TO ME	1	2	3	4	
THE TRIGGER(S) OF MY ILLNESS AND THEIR MEANING(S)	1	2	3	4	
MY FAMILY RELATIONSHIPS BEFORE AND SINCE ANOREXIA	1	2	3	4	
MY SENSE OF SELF: SOCIAL	1	2	3	4	
MY SENSE OF SELF: SEXUAL	1	2	3	4	
THE ORIGINS OF MY ANXIETY	1	2	3	4	
MY USE OF AVOIDANCE TO DEAL WITH CONFLICT	1	2	3	4	
MY FAMILY'S USE OF AVOIDANCE TO DEAL WITH CONFLICT	1	2	3	4	
MY OTHER MOODS	1	2	3	4	
WHY I APPROACH OTHERS IN THE WAY THAT I DO	1	2	3	4	
MY PRESENT OR FUTURE CAREER: WHY I HAVE CHOSEN IT	1	2	3	4	
MY RELATIONSHIPS WITH AUTHORITY	1	2	3	4	
MY IMPULSES AND THE WAY I MANAGE THEM	1	2	3	4	
DIFFICULTIES WITH MY CHOICE OF FOOD	1	2	3	4	
NEW THINGS/SITUATIONS I WOULD LIKE TO TRY	1	2	3	4	
MY DIFFICULTY GAINING/ MAINTAINING WEIGHT	1	2	3	4	
ANY OTHER PROBLEMS (PLEASE SPECIFY)	1	2	3	4	

WE SUGGEST YOU RAISE THESE THINGS IN ANY PART OF THE THERAPY

FOURTH (BEFORE-TARGET WEIGHT) REVIEW (to be discussed with therapist)

DATE ....

MY RATING OF CHANGE IN ME:
1 = More of a problem than ever
2 = No real change
3 = Some improved recognition and understanding of this subject
4 = Much improved recognition and understanding of this subject

	RATING OF CHANGE				INDICATE IF DISCUSSED WITH LOG BOOK PARTNER
THE MEANING OF MY SHAPE TO ME	1	2	3	4	
THE TRIGGER(S) OF MY ILLNESS AND THEIR MEANING(S)	1	2	3	4	
MY FAMILY RELATIONSHIPS BEFORE AND SINCE ANOREXIA	1	2	3	4	
MY SENSE OF SELF: SOCIAL	1	2	3	4	
MY SENSE OF SELF: SEXUAL	1	2	3	4	
THE ORIGINS OF MY ANXIETY	1	2	3	4	
MY USE OF AVOIDANCE TO DEAL WITH CONFLICT	1	2	3	4	
MY FAMILY'S USE OF AVOIDANCE TO DEAL WITH CONFLICT	1	2	3	4	
MY OTHER MOODS	1	2	3	4	
WHY I APPROACH OTHERS IN THE WAY THAT I DO	1	2	3	4	
MY PRESENT OR FUTURE CAREER: WHY I HAVE CHOSEN IT	1	2	3	4	
MY RELATIONSHIPS WITH AUTHORITY	1	2	3	4	
MY IMPULSES AND THE WAY I MANAGE THEM	1	2	3	4	
DIFFICULTIES WITH MY CHOICE OF FOOD	1	2	3	4	
NEW THINGS/SITUATIONS I WOULD LIKE TO TRY	1	2	3	4	
MY DIFFICULTY GAINING/ MAINTAINING WEIGHT	1	2	3	4	
ANY OTHER PROBLEMS (PLEASE SPECIFY)	1	2	3	4	

....

WE SUGGEST YOU RAISE THESE THINGS IN ANY PART OF THE THERAPY

56

BEFORE-TARGET WEIGHT PROBLEMS LIST

DATE: WEIGHT:

Note, in the top row of the boxes below, various circumstances that affect the list of activities as they apply to you. Rate any changes in these experiences since last time, using the rating scale described below and/or add comments if you wish.

1 = More of a problem than ever.   2 = No real change.   3 = Some change in the desired direction.   4 = Much change in the desired direction.

Asserting myself							
Being alone							
Being spontaneous							
Cooking							
Communicating							
Decison making							

BEFORE-TARGET WEIGHT PROBLEMS LIST

DATE: WEIGHT:

Note, in the top row of the boxes below, various circumstances that affect the list of activities as they apply to you. Rate any changes in these experiences since last time, using the rating scale described below and/or add comments if you wish.

1 = More of a problem than ever.   2 = No real change.   3 = Some change in the desired direction.   4 = Much change in the desired direction.

Dietary education + menu planning						
Eating with others						
Expression of feelings						
Feeling in charge of myself						
Having fun						
Indulging myself						

58

BEFORE-TARGET WEIGHT PROBLEMS LIST

DATE: WEIGHT:

Note, in the top row of the boxes below, various circumstances that affect the list of activities as they apply to you. Rate any changes in these experiences since last time, using the rating scale described below and/or add comments if you wish.

1 = More of a problem than ever.   2 = No real change.   3 = Some change in the desired direction.   4 = Much change in the desired direction.

Loving others							
My meanness							
My self-esteem							
Normal exercise							
Owning my sexuality							
Serving normal portions							

BEFORE-TARGET WEIGHT PROBLEMS LIST

DATE: WEIGHT:

Note, in the top row of the boxes below, various circumstances that affect the list of activities as they apply to you. Rate any changes in these experiences since last time, using the rating scale described below and/or add comments if you wish.

1 = More of a problem than ever.   2 = No real change.   3 = Some change in the desired direction.   4 = Much change in the desired direction.

Shopping for clothes/cosmetics etc.							
Shopping + spending money on food							
Socialising							
Thinking of others							
Touching others							
Trusting others							

AT AND AFTER TARGET WEIGHT

We would like to emphasise that the tasks after target weight are different from those before target weight. You are now faced with the task of maintaining your target weight and dealing with the challenges that are to be part of your life. These challenges are to some extent the same problems that previously overwhelmed you and to which your solution was anorexia nervosa. Target weight, though an important achievement (that you may not have thought possible when you started treatment), is only the beginning of the struggle along the road to recovery.

The first step is to consolidate the gains you have made both in terms of:
1) achieving and sustaining your adult weight and,
as importantly,
2) your relationships with yourself and your body,
3) your relationships with others, both in the family and
the broader social sphere.

As in the "before-target weight" section, the following pages are titles of subjects which we believe to be particularly relevant to people with anorexia nervosa. The important question to keep in mind when tackling each heading is how have things changed? Are you or your family different in some way? If this is the case, what are the changes, how do you feel about them, and can you cope with the change?

Once again, we suggest that you briefly record each week your feelings and thoughts about each topic so that you can then come to discuss them with your therapist. You may also wish to continue to use the self-help book and relevant parts of **Let Me Be** or other books, to help you to organise your views.

At the end of the section are pages which are to be used to structure reviews of your progress. At the first review after target weight you probably need to reconsider the goal for each topic against which to rate any change in your recognition and understanding of yourself.

There are also the problem lists similar to the ones in the before-target weight pages and which are intended to continue to help you pinpoint "problems" and look for settings in which these can be tackled.

Continue to date each entry.

Dietetic advice and and continued psychological help and support should buttress your use of this log book. Further useful information at this stage is also contained in the self-help book **Anorexia Nervosa and the Wish to Change**.

THE MEANING OF MY SHAPE TO ME

THE MEANING OF MY SHAPE TO ME

THE TRIGGER(S) OF MY ILLNESS AND THEIR MEANING(S)

THE TRIGGER(S) OF MY ILLNESS AND THEIR MEANING(S)

MY FAMILY (OF ORIGIN) RELATIONSHIPS; BEFORE AND SINCE ANOREXIA

MY FAMILY (OF ORIGIN) RELATIONSHIPS; BEFORE AND SINCE ANOREXIA

MY SENSE OF SELF — SOCIAL

MY SENSE OF SELF — SOCIAL

MY SENSE OF SELF — SEXUAL

MY SENSE OF SELF — SEXUAL

THE ORIGINS OF MY ANXIETY

THE ORIGINS OF MY ANXIETY

MY USE OF AVOIDANCE TO DEAL WITH CONFLICT

MY USE OF AVOIDANCE TO DEAL WITH CONFLICT

MY FAMILY'S USE OF AVOIDANCE TO DEAL WITH CONFLICT

MY FAMILY'S USE OF AVOIDANCE TO DEAL WITH CONFLICT

MY OTHER MOODS

MY OTHER MOODS

WHY I APPROACH OTHERS IN THE WAY THAT I DO

WHY I APPROACH OTHERS IN THE WAY THAT I DO

MY PRESENT OR FUTURE CAREER; WHY I HAVE CHOSEN IT

MY PRESENT OR FUTURE CAREER; WHY I HAVE CHOSEN IT

MY RELATIONSHIPS WITH AUTHORITY

MY RELATIONSHIPS WITH AUTHORITY

MY IMPULSES AND THE WAY I MANAGE THEM

MY IMPULSES AND THE WAY I MANAGE THEM

DIFFICULTIES WITH MY CHOICE OF FOOD

DIFFICULTIES WITH MY CHOICE OF FOOD

NEW THINGS AND/OR SITUATIONS I WOULD LIKE TO TRY AND EXPERIMENT WITH

NEW THINGS AND/OR SITUATIONS I WOULD LIKE TO TRY AND EXPERIMENT WITH

MY DIFFICULTY MAINTAINING MY TARGET WEIGHT

MY DIFFICULTY MAINTAINING MY TARGET WEIGHT

ANY OTHER PROBLEMS
Specify what the problem is:

....

95

ANY OTHER PROBLEMS
Specify what the problem is:

....

ANY OTHER PROBLEMS
Specify what the problem is:

....

ANY OTHER PROBLEMS
Specify what the problem is:

....

98

FIRST (POST-TARGET WEIGHT) REVIEW (to be discussed with therapist)

DATE .... (insert the date for your next review now on the next review sheet)

MY RATING OF CHANGE IN ME:
- 1 = More of a problem than ever
- 2 = No real change
- 3 = Some improved recognition and understanding of this subject
- 4 = Much improved recognition and understanding of this subject

	RATING OF CHANGE				INDICATE IF DISCUSSED WITH LOG BOOK PARTNER
THE MEANING OF MY SHAPE TO ME	1	2	3	4	
THE TRIGGER(S) OF MY ILLNESS AND THEIR MEANING(S)	1	2	3	4	
MY FAMILY RELATIONSHIPS BEFORE AND SINCE ANOREXIA	1	2	3	4	
MY SENSE OF SELF: SOCIAL	1	2	3	4	
MY SENSE OF SELF: SEXUAL	1	2	3	4	
THE ORIGINS OF MY ANXIETY	1	2	3	4	
MY USE OF AVOIDANCE TO DEAL WITH CONFLICT	1	2	3	4	
MY FAMILY'S USE OF AVOIDANCE TO DEAL WITH CONFLICT	1	2	3	4	
MY OTHER MOODS	1	2	3	4	
WHY I APPROACH OTHERS IN THE WAY THAT I DO	1	2	3	4	
MY PRESENT OR FUTURE CAREER: WHY I HAVE CHOSEN IT	1	2	3	4	
MY RELATIONSHIPS WITH AUTHORITY	1	2	3	4	
MY IMPULSES AND THE WAY I MANAGE THEM	1	2	3	4	
DIFFICULTIES WITH MY CHOICE OF FOOD	1	2	3	4	
NEW THINGS/SITUATIONS TO TRY	1	2	3	4	
MY DIFFICULTY MAINTAINING MY TARGET WEIGHT	1	2	3	4	
ANY OTHER PROBLEMS (PLEASE SPECIFY)	1	2	3	4	

....

WE SUGGEST YOU RAISE THESE THINGS IN ANY PART OF THE THERAPY

SECOND (POST-TARGET WEIGHT) REVIEW (to be discussed with therapist)

DATE .... (insert the date for your next review now on the next review sheet)

MY RATING OF CHANGE IN ME:
1 = More of a problem than ever
2 = No real change
3 = Some improved recognition and understanding of this subject
4 = Much improved recognition and understanding of this subject

	RATING OF CHANGE				INDICATE IF DISCUSSED WITH LOG BOOK PARTNER
THE MEANING OF MY SHAPE TO ME	1	2	3	4	
THE TRIGGER(S) OF MY ILLNESS AND THEIR MEANING(S)	1	2	3	4	
MY FAMILY RELATIONSHIPS BEFORE AND SINCE ANOREXIA	1	2	3	4	
MY SENSE OF SELF: SOCIAL	1	2	3	4	
MY SENSE OF SELF: SEXUAL	1	2	3	4	
THE ORIGINS OF MY ANXIETY	1	2	3	4	
MY USE OF AVOIDANCE TO DEAL WITH CONFLICT	1	2	3	4	
MY FAMILY'S USE OF AVOIDANCE TO DEAL WITH CONFLICT	1	2	3	4	
MY OTHER MOODS	1	2	3	4	
WHY I APPROACH OTHERS IN THE WAY THAT I DO	1	2	3	4	
MY PRESENT OR FUTURE CAREER: WHY I HAVE CHOSEN IT	1	2	3	4	
MY RELATIONSHIPS WITH AUTHORITY	1	2	3	4	
MY IMPULSES AND THE WAY I MANAGE THEM	1	2	3	4	
THE REASONS FOR MY DIETETIC DIFFICULTIES, PARTICULARLY DIFFICULTIES WITH CHOICE OF FOOD	1	2	3	4	
ANY OTHER PROBLEMS (PLEASE SPECIFY)	1	2	3	4	
ANY OTHER PROBLEMS (PLEASE SPECIFY)	1	2	3	4	

WE SUGGEST YOU RAISE THESE THINGS IN ANY PART OF THE THERAPY

THIRD (POST-TARGET WEIGHT) REVIEW (to be discussed with therapist)

DATE .... (insert the date for your next review now on the next review sheet)

MY RATING OF CHANGE IN ME: 1 = More of a problem than ever
2 = No real change
3 = Some improved recognition and understanding of this subject
4 = Much improved recognition and understanding of this subject

	RATING OF CHANGE	INDICATE IF DISCUSSED WITH LOG BOOK PARTNER
THE MEANING OF MY SHAPE TO ME	1 2 3 4	
THE TRIGGER(S) OF MY ILLNESS AND THEIR MEANING(S)	1 2 3 4	
MY FAMILY RELATIONSHIPS BEFORE AND SINCE ANOREXIA	1 2 3 4	
MY SENSE OF SELF: SOCIAL	1 2 3 4	
MY SENSE OF SELF: SEXUAL	1 2 3 4	
THE ORIGINS OF MY ANXIETY	1 2 3 4	
MY USE OF AVOIDANCE TO DEAL WITH CONFLICT	1 2 3 4	
MY FAMILY'S USE OF AVOIDANCE TO DEAL WITH CONFLICT	1 2 3 4	
MY OTHER MOODS	1 2 3 4	
WHY I APPROACH OTHERS IN THE WAY THAT I DO	1 2 3 4	
MY PRESENT OR FUTURE CAREER: WHY I HAVE CHOSEN IT	1 2 3 4	
MY RELATIONSHIPS WITH AUTHORITY	1 2 3 4	
MY IMPULSES AND THE WAY I MANAGE THEM	1 2 3 4	
THE REASONS FOR MY DIETETIC DIFFICULTIES, PARTICULARLY DIFFICULTIES WITH CHOICE OF FOOD	1 2 3 4	
ANY OTHER PROBLEMS (PLEASE SPECIFY)	1 2 3 4	
ANY OTHER PROBLEMS (PLEASE SPECIFY)	1 2 3 4	

WE SUGGEST YOU RAISE THESE THINGS IN ANY PART OF THE THERAPY

FOURTH (POST-TARGET WEIGHT) REVIEW (to be discussed with therapist)

DATE ....

MY RATING OF CHANGE IN ME:
1 = More of a problem than ever
2 = No real change
3 = Some improved recognition and understanding of this subject
4 = Much improved recognition and understanding of this subject

	RATING OF CHANGE				INDICATE IF DISCUSSED WITH LOG BOOK PARTNER
THE MEANING OF MY SHAPE TO ME	1	2	3	4	
THE TRIGGER(S) OF MY ILLNESS AND THEIR MEANING(S)	1	2	3	4	
MY FAMILY RELATIONSHIPS BEFORE AND SINCE ANOREXIA	1	2	3	4	
MY SENSE OF SELF: SOCIAL	1	2	3	4	
MY SENSE OF SELF: SEXUAL	1	2	3	4	
THE ORIGINS OF MY ANXIETY	1	2	3	4	
MY USE OF AVOIDANCE TO DEAL WITH CONFLICT	1	2	3	4	
MY FAMILY'S USE OF AVOIDANCE TO DEAL WITH CONFLICT	1	2	3	4	
MY OTHER MOODS	1	2	3	4	
WHY I APPROACH OTHERS IN THE WAY THAT I DO	1	2	3	4	
MY PRESENT OR FUTURE CAREER: WHY I HAVE CHOSEN IT	1	2	3	4	
MY RELATIONSHIPS WITH AUTHORITY	1	2	3	4	
MY IMPULSES AND THE WAY I MANAGE THEM	1	2	3	4	
THE REASONS FOR MY DIETETIC DIFFICULTIES, PARTICULARLY DIFFICULTIES WITH CHOICE OF FOOD	1	2	3	4	
ANY OTHER PROBLEMS (PLEASE SPECIFY)	1	2	3	4	
ANY OTHER PROBLEMS (PLEASE SPECIFY)	1	2	3	4	

WE SUGGEST YOU RAISE THESE THINGS IN ANY PART OF THE THERAPY

POST-TARGET WEIGHT PROBLEMS LIST — No. 1

DATE: WEIGHT:

Note, in the top row of the boxes below, various circumstances that affect the list of activities as they apply to you. Rate any changes in these experiences since last time, using the rating scale described below and/or add comments if you wish.

1 = More of a problem than ever.   2 = No real change.   3 = Some change in the desired direction.   4 = Much change in the desired direction.

Asserting myself							
Being alone							
Being spontaneous							
Cooking							
Communicating							
Decision making							

POST-TARGET WEIGHT PROBLEMS LIST — No. 1

DATE: WEIGHT:

Note, in the top row of the boxes below, various circumstances that affect the list of activities as they apply to you. Rate any changes in these experiences since last time, using the rating scale described below and/or add comments if you wish.

1 = More of a problem than ever.   2 = No real change.   3 = Some change in the desired direction.   4 = Much change in the desired direction.

Dietary education + menu planning							
Eating with others							
Expression of feelings							
Feeling in charge of myself							
Having fun							
Indulging myself							

POST-TARGET WEIGHT PROBLEMS LIST — No. 1

DATE: WEIGHT:

Note, in the top row of the boxes below, various circumstances that affect the list of activities as they apply to you. Rate any changes in these experiences since last time, using the rating scale described below and/or add comments if you wish.

1 = More of a problem than ever.   2 = No real change.   3 = Some change in the desired direction.   4 = Much change in the desired direction.

Loving others							
My meanness							
My self-esteem							
Normal exercise							
Owning my sexuality							
Serving normal portions							

POST-TARGET WEIGHT PROBLEMS LIST — No. 1

DATE: WEIGHT:

Note, in the top row of the boxes below, various circumstances that affect the list of activities as they apply to you. Rate any changes in these experiences since last time, using the rating scale described below and/or add comments if you wish.

1 = More of a problem than ever.   2 = No real change.   3 = Some change in the desired direction.   4 = Much change in the desired direction.

Shopping for clothes/cosmetics etc.							
Shopping + spending money on food							
Socialising							
Thinking of others							
Touching others							
Trusting others							

106

POST-TARGET WEIGHT PROBLEMS LIST — No. 2

DATE: WEIGHT:

Note, in the top row of the boxes below, various circumstances that affect the list of activities as they apply to you. Rate any changes in these
experiences since last time, using the rating scale described below and/or add comments if you wish.

1 = More of a problem than ever.   2 = No real change.   3 = Some change in the desired direction.   4 = Much change in the desired direction.

Asserting myself							
Being alone							
Being spontaneous							
Cooking							
Communicating							
Decision making							

POST-TARGET WEIGHT PROBLEMS LIST — No. 2

DATE:

WEIGHT:

Note, in the top row of the boxes below, various circumstances that affect the list of activities as they apply to you. Rate any changes in these experiences since last time, using the rating scale described below and/or add comments if you wish.

1 = More of a problem than ever.   2 = No real change.   3 = Some change in the desired direction.   4 = Much change in the desired direction.

Dietary education + menu planning						
Eating with others						
Expression of feelings						
Feeling in charge of myself						
Having fun						
Indulging myself						

108

POST-TARGET WEIGHT PROBLEMS LIST — No. 2

DATE: WEIGHT:

Note, in the top row of the boxes below, various circumstances that affect the list of activities as they apply to you. Rate any changes in these experiences since last time, using the rating scale described below and/or add comments if you wish.

1 = More of a problem than ever.　　2 = No real change.　　3 = Some change in the desired direction.　　4 = Much change in the desired direction.

Loving others							
My meanness							
My self-esteem							
Normal exercise							
Owning my sexuality							
Serving normal portions							

POST-TARGET WEIGHT PROBLEMS LIST — No. 2

DATE: WEIGHT:

Note, in the top row of the boxes below, various circumstances that affect the list of activities as they apply to you. Rate any changes in these experiences since last time, using the rating scale described below and/or add comments if you wish.

1 = More of a problem than ever. 2 = No real change. 3 = Some change in the desired direction. 4 = Much change in the desired direction.

Shopping for clothes/cosmetics etc.							
Shopping + spending money on food							
Socialising							
Thinking of others							
Touching others							
Trusting others							

CONTINUED GROWTH, STRUGGLE AND FULFILMENT

The treatment programme you've been involved in, and which incorporates the log book, has now come to the end of its first and most intensive phase. Anorexia nervosa is a very challenging and difficult disorder and recovery takes a number of years. To consolidate and build on your achievements in this initial phase of treatments you will continue to meet for review sessions in the out-patient department. The number of sessions will be in keeping with the original agreed package but also will take into account your clinical condition. You can continue to use the log book by re-reading it from time to time and by using the "diary" pages at the end. During the full course of your involvement in treatment you and your carers may benefit from starting a second log book, using and adapting it according to need. We wish you every success in your courageous endeavours.

The **Eating Disorders Association** is a further appropriate source of support. It is a nationwide organisation which aims to offer help and advice to sufferers and their families. They offer a telephone helpline, answer letters and have a huge list of resources available to people suffering from eating disorders. They also run a network of self-help groups for sufferers and sometimes their families. They publish a regular newsletter for members.

We recommend that you join this organisation if you have not already done so.
The address and telephone number are:

Eating Disorders Association
Sackville Place,
44 Magdalen Street
Norwich,
Norfolk NR3 1JE
Tel: 01603-621414

PERSONAL DIARY

PERSONAL DIARY

PERSONAL DIARY

PERSONAL DIARY

PERSONAL DIARY

PERSONAL DIARY

118

PERSONAL DIARY

PERSONAL DIARY

PERSONAL DIARY

PERSONAL DIARY

PERSONAL DIARY

PERSONAL DIARY

PERSONAL DIARY